new wave MicroWAVE

Food & Styling ANNE MARSHALL
Photography ANDREW ELTON

A J.B. Fairfax Press Publication

INTRODUCTION

Over the years many people have become disillusioned with microwave cooking and often the microwave is used only for a few very specific tasks. This has been largely due to the fact that we have been told and shown all the things that we can cook in the microwave, but not always what the microwave does best. In this book you will only find recipes that save you time or dishes that are every bit as good as if they were cooked conventionally – in fact many are better.

This book is all about showing you how to make the most of your microwave and use it to its full advantage.

EDITORIAL
Food Editor: Rachel Blackmore
Editor: Linda Venturoni
Editorial and Production Assistant: Danielle Thiris
Editorial Coordinator: Margaret Kelly

Photography: Andrew Elton
Food and Styling: Anne Marshall
Food Stylist's Assistant: Ann Bollard

DESIGN AND PRODUCTION
Manager: Sheridan Carter
Senior Production Editor: Anna Maguire
Picture Editor: Kirsten Holmes
Production Editor: Sheridan Packer
Layout and Design: Lulu Dougherty
Cover Design: Michele Withers

Published by J.B. Fairfax Press Pty Limited
80-82 McLachlan Avenue
Rushcutters Bay, NSW 2011, Australia
A.C.N. 003 738 430

Formatted by J.B. Fairfax Press Pty Limited
Printed by Toppan Printing Co, Singapore
PRINTED IN SINGAPORE

JBFP 354
Includes Index
ISBN 1 86343 192 6

DISTRIBUTION AND SALES
Australia: J.B. Fairfax Press Pty Limited
Ph: (02) 361 6366 Fax: (02) 360 6262
United Kingdom: J.B. Fairfax Press Limited
Ph: (01933) 40 2330 Fax: (01933) 40 2234

ABOUT THIS BOOK

INGREDIENTS

Unless otherwise stated the following ingredients are used in this book:

Cream	Double, suitable for whipping
Flour	White flour, plain or standard
Sugar	White sugar

WHAT'S IN A TABLESPOON?

AUSTRALIA
1 tablespoon = 20 mL or 4 teaspoons
NEW ZEALAND
1 tablespoon = 15 mL or 3 teaspoons
UNITED KINGDOM
1 tablespoon = 15 mL or 3 teaspoons
The recipes in this book were tested in Australia where a 20 mL tablespoon is standard. The tablespoon in the New Zealand and the United Kingdom sets of measuring spoons is 15 mL. For recipes using baking powder, gelatine, bicarbonate of soda, small quantities of flour and cornflour, simply add another teaspoon for each tablespoon specified.

CANNED FOODS

Can sizes vary between countries and manufacturers. You may find the quantities in this book are slightly different to what is available. Purchase and use the can size nearest to the suggested size in the recipe.

All the recipes in this book have been tested in a Sharp Microwave Oven with an output power of 900 watts (IEC705 – 1988) or 750 watts (AS2895 – 1986).
The output power of most domestic microwaves ranges between 600 and 900 watts (IEC705 – 1988) or 500 and 800 watts (AS2895 – 1986), so it may be necessary to vary cooking times slightly depending on the output power of your microwave.

CONTENTS

USING THIS BOOK

This cookbook is for the modern cook who likes to use trendy, fashionable ingredients in healthy, nourishing recipes that are quick and easy to prepare. Dishes that are good for you and look great, combined with fresh produce, vegetables, salads and fruit are the goals of the modern new-wave cook of today.

This collection of delicious recipes will inspire you to make the most of your microwave every time you have the need to eat! Everyone uses the microwave for defrosting, reheating and the odd cup of coffee or a bowl of porridge, but these recipes will help you to quickly become the trendiest cook in your neighbourhood.

There are some super ideas for snacks for cooks on the run, sustaining soups for family and friends, main meals to delight the eye and please the palate, a wide variety of tantalising vegetable and grain side dishes for all seasons, desserts to tempt and surprise, and special treats ranging from fruity preserves to chocolate indulgences and party fare. All of them save you time and energy because they are quick to prepare and then cooked in your microwave.

WHY MICROWAVE?
Nearly every microwave cookbook attempts to explain what a microwave is, or what microwave energy is and how it cooks your food. This book suggests that you refer to your microwave direction manual or instruction booklet to demystify these points and prefers instead to inspire you to try this selection of quick and simple recipes.

The microwave can be a great aid in your kitchen as long as you know how to use it. It can melt without mess and defrost diligently, it can start a dish in its first stage or finish it off quickly in its last stage. It cooks fish, chicken and vegetables extraordinarily well and because of the shorter cooking time maximum amounts of nutrients, natural colour and taste are retained. It takes the drama out of melting chocolate and can save time when preserving small quantities of fruit. All this and it helps to keep your kitchen cool in hot weather.

It is an incredible piece of kitchen equipment which many people do not use to its maximum potential. These recipes will have you using your microwave more and not only will you enjoy making them, but you will also enjoy the compliments when you serve delicious food.

EQUIPMENT
It is important to use microwave-safe or microwavable equipment. Use heatproof or 'Pyrex' glassware bowls and jugs, china or pottery plates and bowls without metal-based painted patterns, and special microwave ware. There is no need to rush off to buy lots of expensive new equipment. Just buy a piece when you need it – you will already have lots of suitable microwavable dishes in your basic cooking equipment. Round bowls, dishes and casseroles allow for even cooking. Round ring moulds and round muffin trays are available for cakes and puddings. There are also special pieces such as omelette makers and egg poachers so look out for handy pieces of equipment for your particular needs. When covering bowls, use a plate instead of clear plastic wrap as this is more environmentally friendly.

If you are unsure whether a ceramic, glass or pottery dish is microwavable use the following simple test to check. Place the dish you wish to test in the microwave with a cup of cold water and cook on HIGH (100%) for 1 minute. If at the end of the minute the dish is hot and water is cold the dish is **not** suitable for microwave use. But if the dish is cool and water hot, it is safe to use. If both are warm, the dish can be used for short-term cooking and reheating.

POSITIONING
Positioning is very important for even and quick cooking of food in the microwave. Think 'edge' rather than 'centre' for small containers of

food and liquids and you will get better and quicker results. Detailed directions for correct positioning of foods are given in many of the recipes to guarantee success.

TIMING
The recipes in this book were cooked in a Sharp Microwave Oven with an output power of 900 watts (IEC705 – 1988) or 750 watts (AS2895 – 1986). If your microwave has a different output power to this you may need to adjust the cooking times slightly. The majority of domestic microwaves have output powers ranging between 600 and 900 watts (IEC705 – 1988) or 500 and 800 watts (AS2895 – 1986). The higher the output power of your microwave the quicker it will cook. The output power or wattage output should appear on the manufacturer's plate on the back of your microwave and in the manual that accompanies it. It is always better to undertime rather than overtime – remember you cannot go backwards! Overtiming can result in toughness, dryness or limpness so take care with timing. Careful timing will give you perfect results. When variable cooking times are given always test after the minimum time and add more time if necessary – just as with conventional cooking the size, shape, thickness and temperature of food before you start cooking will all effect the cooking time.

POWER SETTINGS
In this book four power settings are used. They are HIGH (100%), MEDIUM-HIGH (70%), MEDIUM (50%) and DEFROST (30%). If the power settings on your microwave differ from these or you have a greater range refer to the manual and use the power setting that represents the percentage stated. You can assume unless the recipe states otherwise that the same power setting is used for the entire recipe. The power setting is only stated once unless it is necessary to use a different setting for part of the recipe.

SUPER SNACKS

Appetising snacks for 'grazers', such as the ever-popular stuffed potato or colourful pizza, and tasty light meals like nachos, are quick and easy to prepare with the help of your microwave. Also included are delicious pâtés to serve with pre-dinner drinks and tantalising bistro-style rolls and crostata to tempt your tastebuds.

RED ONION AND CHEESE CROSTATA

2 tablespoons olive oil
1 clove garlic, crushed
4 thick slices French bread stick,
diagonally sliced
200 g/6$^1/_2$ oz goat's cheese marinated
in 2 tablespoons French dressing

RED ONION CONFIT
30 g/1 oz butter
2 red onions, thinly sliced
1 teaspoon sugar
$^1/_4$ cup/60 mL/2 fl oz red wine
2 teaspoons balsamic or
red wine vinegar
1 tablespoon chopped thyme or
lemon thyme

1   To make confit, place butter in a microwavable glass or ceramic bowl and melt on MEDIUM (50%) for 2 minutes.

2   Add onions, cover and cook on HIGH (100%) for 4 minutes, stir, then cook for 4 minutes longer. Stir in sugar, wine and vinegar and cook, uncovered, for 5 minutes. Stir in thyme.

3   Combine oil and garlic and brush over one side of each bread slice. Place under a preheated hot grill and cook for 3-4 minutes or until lightly toasted.

4   Cut cheese into thick slices. Place confit on toasted side of each bread slice, top with cheese and serve.

Serves 4

The onion confit stores well in the refrigerator, but should be eaten at room temperature for the best flavour.
For a light meal serve with a salad of mixed lettuce leaves or rocket.

QUICK MEDITERRANEAN PIZZA

1 oval or small round wholemeal
pitta bread
1 teaspoon tomato paste (purée)
$^1/_2$ teaspoon olive paste (pâté)
4 tablespoons thick Napolitana or
similar tomato pasta sauce
60 g/2 oz grated mozzarella cheese
4 segments marinated artichoke hearts
1 teaspoon capers, drained
4 anchovy fillets, drained
1 sun-dried tomato in oil, drained
and sliced
1 tablespoon grated Parmesan cheese

Serves 1

1   Spread pitta bread with tomato paste (purée), then with olive paste (pâté).

2   Place pasta sauce and mozzarella cheese in a bowl and mix to combine. Spread over pitta bread. Arrange artichokes, capers, anchovies and sun-dried tomato attractively on top and sprinkle with Parmesan cheese.

3   Place pizza on a double thickness of absorbent kitchen paper on edge of turntable and cook on MEDIUM (50%) for 2 minutes, turn, then cook for 2 minutes longer.

Using fresh pitta bread and ingredients from the store cupboard and refrigerator this pizza makes a quick snack. The oval-shaped Egyptian variety of pitta bread is the best for even cooking in the microwave.

Tandoori Prawn Rolls

Tandoori Prawn Rolls

3 tablespoons tandoori paste
natural yogurt
12 large uncooked prawns, shelled
and deveined
2 naan bread
4 tablespoons coarsely chopped
cucumber

1 Place tandoori paste and 1 tablespoon yogurt in a bowl and mix to combine. Add prawns and toss to coat. Cover and marinate in the refrigerator for at least 1 hour or up to 24 hours.

2 Place prawns, like numbers on a clock face with the thickest part towards the edge, on a microwavable dinner plate and cook on HIGH (100%) for 1 minute, then on MEDIUM (50%) for 1-2 minutes or until prawns change colour and are cooked.

3 Heat naan bread on DEFROST (30%) for 1 minute. Place 6 prawns along centre of each naan bread, top with cucumber and 2 tablespoons yogurt, roll up and serve immediately.

Serves 2

A delicious snack, perfect for a weekend lunch or supper on the run. The longer you marinate the prawns the more robust the flavour. Take care not to overcook the prawns or they will become tough.

Plate and bowl Arzberg Tray Orson & Blake

THE JACKET BAKED POTATO SNACK

1 x 200 g/6^1/$_2$ oz red-skinned potato

CLASSIC TOPPING
2 tablespoons sour cream
chopped fried bacon
snipped fresh chives or thinly sliced
spring onions

MEXICAN TOPPING
2 teaspoons butter
2 tablespoons bottled tomato salsa or
taco sauce
30 g/1 oz grated tasty cheese
(mature Cheddar)

ITALIAN TOPPING
2 teaspoons olive oil
2 tablespoons Napolitana or similar
tomato pasta sauce
1 tablespoon grated Parmesan cheese

AMERICAN TOPPING
2 teaspoons butter
125 g/4 oz canned creamed sweet corn
30 g/1 oz grated tasty cheese
(mature Cheddar)

SEAFOOD TOPPING
90 g/3 oz canned tuna in oil, drained
and flaked
2 tablespoons sour cream
1 tablespoon red caviar or
lumpfish roe
1 tablespoon black caviar or
lumpfish roe
snipped fresh chives
finely chopped spring onions
chopped fresh parsley

You can save an enormous amount of time by cooking jacket baked potatoes in the microwave instead of in the conventional oven – 5 minutes as compared to 1 hour! The result is not exactly the same as the microwaved potato does not have a crisp skin, however the time saved puts the microwaved jacket baked potato into the category of a quick, economical, healthy and delicious snack. How you top it is only limited by your imagination.

1   Wash potato under cold running water and remove any 'eyes'. Pat dry and using a sharp knife score around the circumference of potato.

2   Place potato on edge of turntable and cook on HIGH (100%) for 3 minutes, turn potato over, then cook for 2 minutes longer.

3   Cut potato in half through the score mark and top with topping of your choice.

For Classic Topping: Top potato halves with sour cream and sprinkle with bacon and chives or spring onions.

For Mexican Topping: Top potato halves with butter, salsa or taco sauce and cheese and cook for 1 minute longer.

For Italian Topping: Sprinkle potato halves with oil, then top with pasta sauce and Parmesan cheese and cook for 1 minute longer.

For American Topping: Top potato halves with butter, sweet corn and cheese and cook for 1 minute longer.

For Seafood Topping: Top potato halves with tuna and cook on MEDIUM (50%) for 1 minute, then top with sour cream, red and black caviar or lumpfish roe, chives, spring onions and parsley.

Serves 1

THAI CHICKEN LAVASH PANCAKES

Lavash bread is a yeast-free bread which is baked in flat sheets. Its history goes back to Biblical times in Syria. It is available from Middle Eastern food shops and some supermarkets. If it is unavailable large pitta bread rounds or naan bread can be used instead. The rolls are delicious served with a snow pea (mangetout) sprout or watercress salad.

1 tablespoon peanut (groundnut) oil
1 clove garlic, crushed
1 teaspoon finely chopped fresh ginger
1 teaspoon finely chopped fresh red chilli
2 boneless chicken breast fillets, cut into thin strips
1 teaspoon chopped fresh coriander root (optional)
1 stalk fresh lemon grass, thinly sliced or $\frac{1}{2}$ teaspoon dried lemon grass, soaked in hot water until soft
2 teaspoons finely grated lime rind
2 tablespoons lime juice
1 tablespoon fish or light soy sauce
2 sheets lavash bread
2 tablespoons chopped fresh coriander
30 g/1 oz bean sprouts
8 cherry tomatoes, quartered

1   Place oil, garlic, ginger and chilli in a microwave browning casserole dish, cover and cook on HIGH (100%) for 2 minutes.

2   Stir in chicken, coriander root, if using, lemon grass, lime rind, lime juice and fish or soy sauce. Push chicken to edges of dish, cover and cook for 2 minutes, stir, then cook for 2 minutes longer.

3   Warm lavash bread on DEFROST (30%) for 1 minute. Stir fresh coriander into chicken mixture and spoon along short end of each sheet of lavash bread, top with bean sprouts and tomatoes, roll up and serve.

Serves 2

Plate Villeroy & Boch *Wooden plate Orson & Blake* Small green bowl *The Bay Tree*

NEAT NACHOS

Left: Thai Chicken Lavash
Pancakes
Above: Neat Nachos

1 large leek, thinly sliced
1 tablespoon olive oil
315 g/10 oz canned red kidney beans,
rinsed and drained
1 cup/250 mL/8 fl oz bottled
taco sauce
60 g/2 oz grated tasty cheese
(mature Cheddar)
125 g/4 oz corn chips
sour cream or prepared guacamole

1   Place leek and oil in a shallow microwavable casserole dish, cover and cook on HIGH (100%) for 2 minutes, stir, then cook for 2 minutes longer.

2   Stir in beans and taco sauce and sprinkle with half the cheese. Cover with corn chips, sprinkle with remaining cheese and cook, uncovered, for 5 minutes. Serve topped with sour cream or guacamole.

Serves 2

This recipe serves two but if you are snacking alone, halve the quantities and make the nachos in an old-fashioned soup plate and reduce the final cooking time to 3 minutes.

15

CHICKEN LIVER PATE

2 onions, diced
2 cloves garlic, crushed
125 g/4 oz butter
500 g/1 lb chicken livers, trimmed
3-4 sprigs fresh parsley
1 teaspoon fresh thyme leaves
1 bay leaf
2 tablespoons brandy or port
warm toast or crispbread
selection of raw vegetables such as
cherry tomatoes, celery sticks, carrot
sticks, broccoli florets, cauliflower
florets and green beans

1   Place onions, garlic and 100 g/3^1/2 oz butter into a microwavable bowl or jug, cover and cook on HIGH (100%) for 4 minutes.

2   Add chicken livers, parsley, thyme, bay leaf and brandy or port to onion mixture, cover and cook for 2 minutes.

Stir well, recover and cook on MEDIUM (50%) for 3 minutes or until livers are just cooked – they should still be pink inside.

3   Remove bay leaf. Place liver mixture in a food processor and process to make a rough pâté. Spoon pâté into a pâté dish or small serving bowl.

4   Place remaining butter in a small microwavable bowl and melt on DEFROST (30%) for 1 minute or until butter is melted. Pour butter over top of pate and chill until required. Serve pâté with toast or crispbread and vegetables.

Serves 6-8

A popular dish to 'snack on' with pre-dinner drinks, pâté is also great for picnics.

SMOKED FISH PATE

250 g/ 8 oz smoked cod or haddock
2 cups/500 mL/16 fl oz boiling water
2 cups/500 mL/16 fl oz milk
1 tablespoon capers, drained
2 tablespoons cream (double)
2 tablespoons lemon juice
2 teaspoons Dijon mustard
freshly ground black pepper
2 tablespoons coarsely chopped
pistachio nuts
1 tablespoon snipped fresh chives

1   Place fish in a microwavable shallow dish, pour over boiling water, cover and cook on HIGH (100%) for 1 minute. Drain off water.

2   Pour milk over fish, cover and cook on MEDIUM (50%) for 5-6 minutes or until fish flakes when tested with a fork. Drain off milk, remove skin and bones from fish and flake flesh.

3   Place fish in a food processor, add capers, cream, lemon juice, mustard and black pepper to taste and process to make a pâté. Stir in pistachio nuts and chives and spoon pâté into a pâté dish or serving bowl. Cover and chill until ready to serve.

Serves 6-8

Kipper fillets are also suitable to use for this recipe but delete step 2 as the fish is already cooked. For a special occasion, serve pâté topped with soft-boiled quail eggs, garnished with chives and accompanied by toasted rye bread or rye crispbread. The milk used for cooking the fish can be reserved and used in a fish sauce or soup, however be sure to use it within 2 days.

Chicken Liver Pâté, Smoked Fish Pâté

SOUPS TO SATISFY

Nutritious and delicious soups can be made quickly in the microwave, cutting down on both cooking time and steam in your kitchen. These recipes are surprisingly quick and convenient, making use of the food processor for chopping and puréeing, the kettle for instant boiling stock, and of course your microwave.

SPICY LAKSA

8 large spring onions, thinly sliced
1 clove garlic, crushed
1 tablespoon peanut (groundnut) oil
3 cups/750 mL/1^1/$_4$ pt boiling
vegetable or chicken stock, made
with stock cubes
1 cup/250 mL/8 fl oz coconut milk
2 tablespoons chilli sauce
1 tablespoon sweet chilli sauce
1 tablespoon crunchy peanut butter
155 g/5 oz quick-cooking noodles
fresh coriander leaves
bean sprouts

1   Place spring onions, garlic and oil in a microwavable bowl or jug, cover and cook on HIGH (100%) for 1 minute.

2   Stir in stock, coconut milk, chilli sauce, sweet chilli sauce and peanut butter, cover and cook for 10 minutes.

3   Stir in noodles, cover and cook for 2 minutes, stir, then cook for 2 minutes longer. Ladle soup into warm soup bowls, sprinkle with coriander and bean sprouts and serve.

Serves 4

This popular Malaysian soup makes a satisfying and delicious meal and is surprisingly quick and easy to make in the microwave.

HOT AND SOUR SOUP

6 large uncooked prawns, shelled and
deveined, shells reserved
2 cups/500 mL/16 fl oz water
2 cups/500 mL/16 fl oz boiling
vegetable stock, made with
stock cubes
^{1}/$_4$ cup/60 mL/2 fl oz lime juice
2 tablespoons fish sauce
1 tablespoon sweet chilli sauce
4 spring onions, thinly sliced
1 tablespoon thinly sliced fresh lemon
grass or 1 teaspoon dried lemon grass,
soaked in hot water until soft
1 tablespoon shredded fresh coriander
2 cloves garlic, crushed
1 teaspoon finely chopped fresh ginger
1 fresh red chilli, seeded and thinly
sliced
1 teaspoon finely chopped coriander
stalks
4 lemon or kaffir lime leaves,
shredded (optional)
whole fresh coriander leaves

1   Place prawn shells and water in a microwavable bowl or jug, cover and cook on HIGH (100%) for 6 minutes. Strain, discard prawn shells and return liquid to a clean bowl or jug.

2   Stir in stock, lime juice, fish sauce, chilli sauce, spring onions, lemon grass, shredded coriander, garlic, ginger, chilli, coriander stalks and lemon or lime leaves, if using, cover and cook for 5 minutes.

3   Cut prawns in half lengthwise, add to soup, cover and cook for 1^1/$_2$ minutes or until prawns change colour and are just cooked. Sprinkle soup with coriander leaves and serve immediately.

Serves 4

This is a microwave version of the famous Thai soup which has many regional versions in Thailand.

Ham and Vegetable Chowder

Ham and Vegetable Chowder

15 g/¹/₂ oz butter
1 onion, finely chopped
2 carrots, diced
1 stalk celery, sliced
3 potatoes, about 350 g/11 oz, cubed
3 cups/750 mL/1¹/₄ pt hot vegetable
or chicken stock, made with
stock cubes
2 tablespoons flour
2 cups/500 mL/16 fl oz milk
250 g/8 oz canned sweet corn kernels,
drained
125 g/4 oz thickly sliced ham, cubed
3 tablespoons chopped fresh parsley
cayenne pepper

Serves 6

1   Place butter and onion in a large microwavable bowl or jug, cover and cook on HIGH (100%) for 3 minutes. Stir in carrots and celery, cover and cook for 3 minutes longer.

2   Add potatoes and 1 cup/250 mL/8 fl oz stock, cover and cook for 5 minutes.

3   Blend flour with 4 tablespoons milk to make a smooth paste. Stir flour mixture and 1 cup/250 mL/8 fl oz milk into soup, cover and cook for 3 minutes.

4   Stir sweet corn, ham and remaining stock and milk into soup, cover and cook for 8 minutes or until soup boils and potatoes are tender. Stir in parsley and sprinkle with cayenne pepper to taste.

Served with crisp cracker biscuits or warm corn bread this thick chunky soup is a meal in itself.

Soup plate Janet Niven Antiques

RED LENTIL AND LEMON SOUP

1 large onion, finely chopped
2 cloves garlic, crushed
1 tablespoon olive oil
200 g/6^1/$_2$ oz red lentils
1 carrot, grated
1 teaspoon ground cumin
3^1/$_2$ cups/875 mL/1^1/$_2$ pt boiling
vegetable or chicken stock, made
with stock cubes
1 stalk celery, thinly sliced
2 tablespoons lemon juice
shredded fresh flat-leafed parsley
lemon wedges (optional)

1   Place onion, garlic and oil in a
microwavable bowl or jug, cover and
cook on HIGH (100%) for 2 minutes,
stir, then cook for 2 minutes longer.

2   Stir in lentils, carrot, cumin and
2 cups/500 mL/16 fl oz stock, cover
and cook for 8 minutes.

3   Mash lentils or purée mixture and
stir in celery, lemon juice, and
remaining stock, cover and cook for
8 minutes or until lentils are tender.
Sprinkle with parsley and serve with
lemon wedges to squeeze into soup, if
desired.

Serves 4

The lemon juice in this thick,
nourishing soup is a
protection against those
winter shivers.

AFRICAN SPICED BEAN SOUP

1 large onion, finely chopped
1 tablespoon olive or peanut
(groundnut) oil
^{1}/$_2$ teaspoon chilli powder
^{1}/$_4$ teaspoon ground cinnamon
440 g/14 oz canned red kidney beans
or black-eyed peas, rinsed and drained
2 tomatoes, chopped
2 cups/500mL/16 fl oz boiling
vegetable stock, made with
stock cubes
1 tablespoon chopped fresh parsley
lemon wedges (optional)

1   Place onion and oil in a
microwavable bowl, cover and cook
on HIGH (100%) for 3 minutes. Stir
in chilli powder and cinnamon.

2   Mash half the beans or peas. Stir
mashed beans or peas, whole beans or
peas, tomatoes, stock and parsley into
onion mixture, cover and cook for
5 minutes.

3   Serve with lemon wedges to squeeze
into soup, if desired.

Serves 4

The food processor is ideal
for finely chopping onions,
it does it in next to no time,
without tears and they cook
more quickly.
Serve this tasty, nourishing
soup with warm bread rolls.

Red Lentil and Lemon Soup,
African Spiced Bean Soup

VICHYSSOISE

4 thin or 2 large leeks, white
parts only, sliced
1 large onion, finely chopped
30 g/1 oz butter
2 potatoes, peeled and thinly sliced
1 stalk celery, thinly sliced
1 tablespoon chopped fresh parsley
4 cups/1 litre/1^3/4 pt boiling chicken
stock, made with stock cubes
1^1/4 cups/315 mL/10 fl oz cream
(double) or light sour cream
freshly ground white pepper
chopped fresh parsley
snipped fresh chives

This classic chilled soup is
easy to prepare in the
microwave keeping the
kitchen cool in hot weather.
In cold weather it is equally
delicious served hot.

1   Place leeks, onion and butter in a
microwavable bowl or jug, cover and
cook on HIGH (100%) for 4 minutes,
stir, then cook for 4 minutes longer.

2   Add potatoes, celery, parsley and
half the stock, cover and cook for
5 minutes, stir, then cook for 5 minutes
longer or until potatoes are tender.

3   Set soup aside to cool slightly, then
purée in a food processor or blender.
Return soup to a clean bowl or jug, stir
in cream or sour cream, remaining
stock and white pepper to taste.

4   To serve cold, set aside to cool, then
cover and chill well. To serve hot, cook
on HIGH (100%) for 10 minutes or
until soup is hot. Just prior to serving,
sprinkle with parsley and chives.

Serves 6

CARROT AND TOMATO SOUP

500 g/1 lb carrots, sliced
440 g/14 oz canned tomatoes,
undrained and mashed
1 onion, finely chopped
1 clove garlic, crushed
2 tablespoons olive oil
3 cups/750 mL/1^1/4 pt boiling chicken
stock, made with stock cubes
^{1}/4 teaspoon ground nutmeg
^{1}/2 cup /125 mL/4 fl oz cream (single)
freshly ground black pepper
chopped fresh parsley
thin strips lime or lemon rind

1   Place carrots in a clean microwavable
plastic bag. Twist neck of bag and fold
under carrots to seal. Place bag on edge
of turntable, patting carrots into an
even layer and cook on HIGH (100%)
for 5-6 minutes or until carrots are
tender. Set aside to cool slightly.

2   Place carrots and tomatoes in a food
processor or blender and purée.

3   Place onion, garlic and oil in a
microwavable bowl or jug, cover and
cook on HIGH (100%) for 2 minutes,
stir, then cook for 2 minutes longer.
Add 1 cup/ 250 mL/8 fl oz stock, cover
and cook for 5 minutes.

4   Stir in carrot mixture, nutmeg and
remaining stock, cover and cook for
8 minutes or until soup is hot.

5   Stir in cream and black pepper to
taste. Sprinkle with parsley and lime or
lemon rind and serve immediately.

Serves 6

Serve with warm French
bread.

Vichyssoise, Carrot and Tomato Soup

BROCCOLI AND ALMOND SOUP

500 g/1 lb broccoli, cut into
small florets
1 large onion, finely chopped
30 g/1 oz butter
4 cups /1 litre/1³/4 pt boiling vegetable
stock, made with stock cubes
1 tablespoon lemon juice
4 tablespoons ground almonds

The ground almonds can be omitted from this recipe if you wish, but they do add a rich flavour and act as a thickening ingredient. Delicious served with toasted wholemeal or herb bread.

1   Wash broccoli under cold running water, shake off excess water and place in a clean microwavable plastic bag. Twist neck of bag and fold under broccoli to seal. Place on edge of turntable and cook on HIGH (100%) for 5-6 minutes or until broccoli is tender. Cool slightly, then place in a food processor or blender and purée.

2   Place onion and butter in a microwavable bowl or jug and cook on HIGH (100%) for 2 minutes, stir, then cook for 2 minutes longer.

3   Stir in 2 cups/500 mL/16 fl oz stock, cover and cook for 5 minutes. Stir in broccoli purée and remaining stock and cook for 5 minutes longer.

4   Add lemon juice and almonds, cook for 1 minute and serve immediately.

Serves 6

BLUSHING VEGETABLE SOUP

3 beetroot, peeled and quartered
500 g/1 lb zucchini (courgettes)
1 onion, finely chopped
1 rasher bacon, chopped
15 g/¹/2 oz butter
6 cups/1.5 litres/2¹/2 pt boiling
chicken or vegetable stock, made
with stock cubes
freshly ground black pepper
6 tablespoons sour cream
chopped fresh herbs of your choice

The rich colour of beetroot gives this delicious soup its pretty blush.

1   Place beetroot in a clean microwavable plastic bag. Twist neck of bag and fold under beetroot to seal. Place bag on edge of turntable and cook on HIGH (100%) for 6-8 minutes or until beetroot are tender. Cool slightly.

2   Place zucchini (courgettes) in a second microwavable plastic bag and secure as for beetroot. Cook for 6-8 minutes or until zucchini (courgettes) are tender. Cool slightly.

3   Place beetroot and zucchini (courgettes) in a food processor and process to finely chop.

4   Place onion, bacon and butter in a microwavable bowl and cook on HIGH (100%) for 2 minutes, stir, then cook for 2 minutes longer. Add vegetable mixture, stock and black pepper to taste, cover and cook for 5-8 minutes or until soup is hot.

5   Ladle soup into warm serving bowls, stir 1 tablespoon sour cream into each bowl and sprinkle with herbs.

Serves 6

*Broccoli and Almond Soup,
Blushing Vegetable Soup*

MAIN MEALS WITH FLAIR

These diverse main meals are sure to delight family and friends. The selection of fish dishes shows just how well this food cooks in the microwave while retaining its natural flavour and delicate texture. You will also find a range of recipes for small cuts of chicken and meat cooked with liquid, minced meat, small birds and even-shaped joints.

SPICY THAI PRAWNS

6 spring onions, sliced diagonally
1 clove garlic, crushed
1 teaspoon finely chopped fresh ginger
1 tablespoon peanut (groundnut) oil
1 teaspoon finely grated lime rind
1 tablespoon lime juice
1 stalk fresh lemon grass, thinly sliced
or $1/2$ teaspoon dried lemon grass,
soaked in hot water until soft
1 tablespoon chopped fresh coriander
1 teaspoon finely chopped fresh
coriander root (optional)
1 fresh red chilli, thinly sliced
$1/2$ cup/125 mL/4 fl oz coconut milk
$1/2$ cup/125 mL/4 fl oz vegetable stock
500 g/1 lb uncooked prawns, shelled
and deveined and halved lengthwise
60 g/2 oz snow peas (mangetout)

1   Place spring onions, garlic, ginger
and oil in a microwavable casserole,
cover and cook on HIGH (100%) for
2 minutes.

2   Add lime rind, lime juice, lemon
grass, fresh coriander, coriander root, if
using, chilli, coconut milk and stock,
cover and cook for 2 minutes.

3   Place prawns around edge of casserole
and place snow peas (mangetout) in
centre. Cover and cook on MEDIUM
(50%) for 1 minute, stir carefully
keeping prawns to the outside and
snow peas (mangetout) in the centre,
then cook for 1 minute longer. Stir
again and cook for 1 minute or until
prawns change colour and are cooked.

Serves 4

This easy Oriental dish only
takes 7 minutes to cook
and is delicious served over
freshly cooked noodles.

THAI-STYLE TROUT

2 small whole trout, cleaned
freshly ground black pepper
2 tablespoons white wine or lemon juice

HERB SAUCE
1 stalk lemon grass, thinly sliced or
$1/2$ teaspoon dried lemon grass, soaked
in hot water until soft
2 kaffir lime leaves or lemon leaves,
thinly sliced (optional)
1 tablespoon chopped spring onion
1 tablespoon chopped fresh coriander
1 tablespoon chopped fresh mint
2 tablespoons lime or lemon juice
2 tablespoons fish sauce

1   Wash trout in cold salted water,
drain and pat dry with absorbent
kitchen paper. Using a sharp knife,
score both sides of trout three times.

2   Lightly oil microwave turntable and
place trout on opposite sides with open
cavity facing towards centre. Season
cavities of trout with black pepper.
Sprinkle wine or lemon juice in
cavities and over trout. Cook on HIGH
(100%) for 5 minutes or until flesh
flakes when tested with a fork.

3   To make sauce, place lemon grass,
lime or lemon leaves, if using, spring
onion, coriander, mint, lime or lemon
juice and fish sauce in a bowl or jug and
mix to combine.

4   To serve, transfer trout to serving
plates and spoon over sauce.

Serves 2

The cooking time for the
trout will vary according to
their size, if they are not
cooked after 5 minutes
reduce the power setting
to MEDIUM (50%) and cook
for 1-2 minutes – this will
prevent overcooking of the
thinner areas.
For a complete meal serve
with rice or warm bread
and a lettuce salad.
Food can be cooked
straight on the turntable, this
is a useful way of cooking
oddly shaped or larger
items such as whole fish
and it saves on washing up.

Provençal-style Scallops

PROVENÇAL-STYLE SCALLOPS

2 carrots, cut into thin strips
250 g/8 oz asparagus or young green
beans, trimmed
375 g/12 oz scallops, cleaned
30 g/1 oz butter
3 spring onions, sliced
2 teaspoons cornflour blended with
$^{1}/_{2}$ cup/125 mL/4 fl oz dry white wine
2 tablespoons lemon juice
1 tablespoon snipped fresh chives

1   Place carrots and asparagus or beans in a clean microwavable plastic bag. Twist neck of bag and fold under vegetables to seal. Place bag on edge of turntable, patting into an even layer and cook on HIGH (100%) for 3 minutes or until vegetables are just cooked. Set aside.

2   Rinse scallops under cold running water and drain well. Set aside.

3   Place butter and spring onions in a shallow microwavable dish and cook on HIGH (100%) for 1 minute.

4   Stir cornflour mixture, lemon juice and chives into butter mixture. Arrange scallops around edge of dish in a single layer, cover and cook on MEDIUM (50%) for 2 minutes, stir carefully keeping scallops to outside edge of dish, then cook for 2 minutes longer.

5   Stir carrots and asparagus or beans into scallop mixture and serve immediately.

Serves 4

For a complete meal serve with lemon-flavoured rice or tiny new potatoes.

Plate Villeroy & Boch

WHOLE FISH WITH CHILLI SAUCE

1 whole firm-fleshed fish, such as
snapper or bream, weighing
500-750 g/1-1^1/$_2$ lb, cleaned
^{1}/$_3$ cup/90 mL/3 fl oz mirin or rice wine
^{1}/$_4$ cup/60 mL/2 fl oz peanut
(groundnut) oil
4 fresh red chillies, seeded and sliced
2 cloves garlic, crushed
^{1}/$_2$ red pepper, sliced
^{1}/$_2$ green pepper, sliced
1 teaspoon brown sugar
3 tablespoons shredded fresh basil
^{1}/$_4$ cup/60 mL/2 fl oz fish sauce
whole basil leaves

The firm moist flesh of the whole fish contrasts well with the textured hot sauce in this easy recipe.
For a complete meal serve with white or brown rice and a green vegetable of your choice.

1 Wash fish under cold running water and pat dry with absorbent kitchen paper. Using a sharp knife, score both sides of fish three times.

2 Place fish on a round microwavable serving plate, sprinkle with mirin or rice wine, cover and cook on MEDIUM (50%) for 8-10 minutes or until flesh flakes when tested with a fork.

3 Place oil, chillies and garlic in a microwavable bowl, cover and cook on HIGH (100%) for 2 minutes.

4 Add red pepper, green pepper, sugar, basil and fish sauce to chilli mixture, mix to combine, cover and cook for 3 minutes. Stir well, then spoon hot sauce over fish, garnish with basil leaves and serve immediately.

Serves 2

BALINESE PRAWN SATAY

14 spring onions
6 shallots, peeled
1 fresh red chilli, seeded
1 teaspoon sliced fresh ginger
1 teaspoon sliced fresh lemon grass
2 sun-dried tomatoes in oil, well
drained and chopped
1 tomato, halved
2 tablespoons peanut (groundnut) oil
2 tablespoons lime juice
16 large uncooked prawns, shelled
and deveined

Allow at least 1 hour to marinate the prawns for a delicious result which is simple and non-messy to cook. Serve prawn satays with rice and a cucumber and tomato salad.
The shallots used in this recipe are the French échalote.

1 Cut 6 spring onions into 2 cm/^{3}/$_4$ in lengths and place in a food processor or blender. Add shallots, chilli, ginger, lemon grass and sun-dried tomatoes and process to finely chop.

2 Remove seeds from tomato, by holding halves in the palm of your hand and squeezing, then dice flesh.

3 Heat oil in a shallow microwavable dish on HIGH (100%) for 2 minutes. Stir in spring onion mixture, cover and cook for 1 minute.

4 Add lime juice, tomato and prawns, mix to combine, cover and marinate for at least 1 hour.

5 Cut remaining spring onions into 2 cm/^{3}/$_4$ in lengths. Drain prawns and thread 2 prawns and 2 pieces of spring onion onto a bamboo skewer. Repeat with remaining prawns and spring onions to make eight skewers. Place four skewers round edge of turntable and cook on MEDIUM (50%) for 1-1^1/$_2$ minutes or until prawns change colour and are cooked. Repeat with remaining skewers. Serve immediately.

Serves 4

Whole Fish with Chilli Sauce,
Balinese Prawn Satay

FISH CUTLETS WITH PESTO

2 large tomatoes, thinly sliced
2 teaspoons balsamic vinegar
2 fish cutlets, such as jewfish,
snapper or salmon
2 tablespoons white wine

PESTO SAUCE
1 bunch fresh basil
2 tablespoons pine nuts
1 clove garlic, peeled and halved
1/4 cup/60 mL/2 fl oz olive oil
4 tablespoons grated Parmesan cheese

1   To make sauce, place basil, pine nuts, garlic and oil in a food processor or blender and process to make a smooth paste. Add Parmesan cheese and process to combine.

2   Arrange tomatoes, slightly overlapping, in a lightly oiled shallow microwavable dish to form a 'base' for each fish cutlet. Sprinkle with vinegar.

3   Place fish cutlets on top of tomatoes, pour over wine, cover and cook on HIGH (100%) for 2 minutes, then on MEDIUM (50%) for 4 minutes.

4   Spoon 2 tablespoons sauce over each cutlet and serve immediately.

Serves 2

Serve with lemon buttered rice and a green vegetable of your choice.
Store leftover pesto in an airtight container in the refrigerator and use as a quick topping for pasta or as a sandwich spread in place of butter.
A good quality commercial pesto could be used to save time or when fresh basil is unavailable.

Plate Orson & Blake *Placemat* Art House

34

Plate Janet Niven Antiques *Bowl* Orson & Blake

FISH AND TOMATO CURRY

Left: Fish Cutlets with Pesto
Above: Fish and Tomato Curry

500 g/1 lb mullet, herring or gemfish
fillets, boned and skinned
2 tablespoons peanut (groundnut) oil
1 teaspoon mustard seeds
1 teaspoon dried fenugreek
1 white onion, cut in 12 wedges
1 teaspoon finely chopped fresh ginger
1 clove garlic, crushed
2 tablespoons curry paste
1 large tomato, cut in wedges
1 cup/200 g/6$^{1}/_{2}$ oz natural yogurt

1   Wash fish and pat dry with absorbent kitchen paper, then cut into 5 cm/2 in pieces.

2   Heat a microwave browning casserole dish on HIGH (100%) for 3 minutes, add oil, mustard seeds and fenugreek, cover and cook for 2 minutes – some of the seeds will pop.

3   Stir in onion, ginger and garlic, cover and cook for 2 minutes longer. Add curry paste and mix to combine. Place fish around edge of dish, top with tomato and place yogurt in centre of dish. Cover and cook for 3 minutes. Turn fish, cover and cook on MEDIUM (50%) for 2 minutes, stir, then cook for 2 minutes longer or until fish is cooked.

Serves 4

This curry has a delicious taste and is a good way to make use of less expensive oily fish such as gemfish, mullet or herring.
Serve with rice, mango chutney and your favourite curry accompaniments.

Plate Accoutrement *Placemat Art House*

Above: Fish Fillets in Yogurt Marinade
Right: Fish Fillets in Grape Jus

FISH FILLETS IN YOGURT MARINADE

2 fillets cod or similar fish, skinned

YOGURT CHILLI MARINADE
$^2/_3$ cup/140 g/4$^1/_2$ oz natural yogurt
2 tablespoons sweet chilli sauce
2 tablespoons chopped fresh coriander
1 fresh red chilli, seeded and finely chopped

Delicious served with savoury couscous, snow peas (mangetout) and carrots.

1   To make marinade, place yogurt, chilli sauce, coriander and chilli in a bowl and mix to combine. Place fish fillets in a shallow glass or ceramic dish, spoon over marinade, cover and marinate in the refrigerator for at least 3 hours.

2   Place fish in a shallow microwavable dish, with thickest parts of fillets towards edge of dish. Spoon over any remaining marinade, cover and cook on MEDIUM (50%) for 4 minutes. To serve, place fillets on serving plates, stir sauce and spoon over fish.

Serves 2

FISH FILLETS IN GRAPE JUS

250 g/8 oz red or black grapes
30 g/1oz butter
2 spring onions, sliced
4 thin white fish fillets, such as John
Dory, whiting or flounder, skinned
1 carrot, cut into thin strips
freshly ground black pepper

1   Place grapes in a food processor or blender and process to make a purée. Push purée through a seive. Discard seeds and skins.

2   Place butter and spring onions in a shallow microwavable dish, cover and cook on HIGH (100%) for 1 minute. Stir well.

3   Place a fish fillet along each edge of dish and fold thinner parts under fillet to make an even thickness. Cover and cook for 2 minutes.

4   Pour grape 'jus' over fish, place carrot in centre of dish and season to taste with black pepper. Cover and cook on MEDIUM (50%) for 3 minutes or until fish is cooked.

Serves 4

Serve with buttered rice or small new potatoes and a salad of mixed salad greens.

Plate The Bay Tree Glass Opus

CHINESE CHICKEN WITH CASHEWS

2 tablespoons peanut (groundnut) oil
1 large onion, cut in 12 wedges
1 clove garlic, crushed
1 teaspoon finely chopped fresh ginger
2 boneless chicken breast fillets, cut
into thin strips
250 g/8 oz broccoli, broken into
small florets
1 carrot, diagonally sliced
1 red pepper, thinly sliced
1 cup/250 mL/8 fl oz plum sauce
60 g /2 oz roasted unsalted cashews

Delicious served with fragrant Jasmine or basmati rice.

1 Place oil, onion, garlic and ginger in a microwave browning casserole dish, cover and cook on HIGH (100%) for 3 minutes.

2 Add chicken, cover and cook for 2 minutes. Add broccoli, carrot, red pepper and plum sauce, stir well, cover and cook for 6 minutes or until vegetables are tender crisp. Sprinkle with cashews and serve immediately.

Serves 4

CHICKEN CURRY

1 tablespoon peanut (groundnut) oil
1 onion, finely chopped
2 boneless chicken breast fillets,
trimmed and halved
2 boneless chicken thighs, trimmed
and halved
2 tablespoons curry paste
1 carrot, thinly sliced
2 tablespoons crunchy peanut butter
440 g/14 oz canned tomatoes,
undrained and mashed
1 chicken stock cube, crumbled
125 g/4 oz green beans, sliced
2 tablespoons cream (double)

Quick and easy to make and delicious to eat! Serve with Indian bread, pappadums and curry accompaniments. Pappadums are easy to cook in the microwave. Place pappadums on absorbent kitchen paper and cook on HIGH (100%) for 1$\frac{1}{2}$-2 minutes or until pappadums puff up and are crisp, turn over and cook for 1-1$\frac{1}{2}$ minutes longer.

1 Place oil and onion in a microwavable casserole dish, cover and cook on HIGH (100%) for 2 minutes.

2 Place chicken around edge of dish and stir curry paste into centre. Add carrot to centre of dish, cover and cook for 3 minutes.

3 Stir in peanut butter, tomatoes and stock cube, cover and cook for 5 minutes longer.

4 Add green beans, stir, cover and cook on MEDIUM (50%) for 10 minutes or until vegetables and chicken are cooked. Stir in cream and serve.

Serves 4

Chicken Curry, Chinese Chicken with Cashews

CHICKEN WITH SWEET POTATOES

500 g/1 lb boneless chicken breast or
thigh fillets, halved
500 g/1 lb orange sweet potatoes, cut
into 2 cm/³/4 in cubes
2 cloves garlic, crushed
2 tablespoons olive oil
1 tablespoon cider or white
wine vinegar
1¹/2 cups/375 mL/12 fl oz bottled
tomato salsa or taco sauce
¹/2 cup/125 mL/4 fl oz chicken stock
¹/2 red pepper, sliced
¹/2 green pepper, sliced

1   Place chicken and sweet potatoes
in a microwavable casserole dish.
Place garlic, oil and vinegar in a bowl,
mix to combine and pour over chicken.
Cover and cook on HIGH (100%) for
5 minutes.

2   Stir in salsa or taco sauce and stock,
cover and cook on MEDIUM (50%)
for 7 minutes. Stir in red and green
pepper and cook for 8 minutes longer.

Serves 4

Use a good quality
processed mild, medium or
hot salsa or taco sauce, for
this easy chicken dish.
Serve with rice and sweet
corn or corn bread.

ORIENTAL POUSSIN

2 x 750 g/1¹/₂ lb poussin or
spatchcock
60 g/2 oz butter, softened
1 bunch fresh coriander, leaves and
roots (optional), chopped
2 teaspoons finely chopped fresh
lemon grass or 1 teaspoon finely
grated lemon rind
¹/₄ teaspoon five spice powder
2 tablespoons peanut (groundnut) oil
1 tablespoon sweet chilli sauce
1 tablespoon light soy sauce

1   Using your fingertips and working
from the neck end of each bird, gently
separate skin on breast from flesh.

2   Place butter, coriander leaves,
coriander roots, if using, lemon grass or
lemon rind and five spice powder in a
bowl and beat to combine.

3   Divide savoury butter in half and
gently push between skin and breast
meat on either side of breast bone,
patting to form an even layer. Truss
birds neatly by tying legs together with
kitchen string and twisting wings under
back.

4   Heat a large microwave browning
dish on HIGH (100%) for 3 minutes.
Add oil and birds, breast down, and
move birds around dish to brown as
much as possible. Remove birds and
place a microwavable roasting rack in
the dish. Place birds on rack.

5   Combine chilli sauce and soy
sauce and brush over birds. Cook on
HIGH (100%) for 5 minutes, then on
MEDIUM (50%) for 5 minutes, brush
with pan juices and cook for 5 minutes
longer.

6   Brush breasts of birds with pan
juices, then cover with 'microwave
pastry crisping and browning wrap'
and secure with wooden toothpicks
or cocktail sticks and cook for
12-15 minutes longer or until birds are
cooked. Stand for 5 minutes.

Serves 2-4

The breasts are covered
with 'microwave pastry
crisping and browning
wrap' to help achieve a
golden colour. If this wrap is
unavailable the birds can
be cooked without it,
however they may not be
quite as brown.
For a complete meal serve
with lemon-flavoured rice
and stir-fried vegetables.

*Left: Chicken with Sweet Potatoes
Right: Oriental Poussin*

Plates Villeroy & Boch Wooden tray Orson & Blake

LAMB AND SPINACH CURRY

2 tablespoons peanut (groundnut) oil
500 g/1 lb cubed shoulder or leg lamb
2 white onions, finely chopped
4 tablespoons mild curry paste
440 g/14 oz canned tomatoes,
undrained and mashed
250 g/8 oz frozen spinach, thawed
and drained
155 mL/5 fl oz coconut milk
2 tablespoons natural yogurt

For a complete meal serve
with rice and your favourite
curry accompaniments.
Ask your butcher for some
tender well-trimmed lamb
for this delicious curry.

1   Heat a microwave browning casserole
dish on HIGH (100%) for 2 minutes.
Add oil, lamb and onions and stir well.
Cover and cook for 2 minutes, stir,
then cook for 2 minutes longer.

2   Stir in curry paste, cover and cook
for 30 seconds. Stir in tomatoes,
spinach and coconut milk, cover and
cook for 5 minutes. Stir and cook on
MEDIUM (50%) for 5 minutes or until
lamb is cooked. Stir in yogurt, cover
and stand for 5 minutes.

Serves 4

STUFFED LOIN OF LAMB

1 x 500 g/1 lb boned and rolled loin
of lamb, trimmed of all visible fat

SPINACH STUFFING
15 g/^{1}/$_2$ oz butter
8 spring onions, thinly sliced
125 g/4 oz cooked spinach,
well drained
1 slice wholemeal bread, crumbed
freshly ground black pepper

MUSTARD GLAZE
1 tablespoon wholegrain mustard
1 tablespoon barbecue sauce
1 tablespoon tomato sauce

Select symetrically shaped
joints without bones for
even cooking and trim off
as much fat as possible. A
marinade or glaze helps to
give the meat an appetising
appearance.
Serve lamb with mint jelly or
sauce, carrots and creamy
mashed potatoes.

1   To make stuffing, place butter and
spring onions in a small microwavable
bowl, cover with a piece of absorbent
kitchen paper and cook on HIGH
(100%) for 2 minutes. Add spinach,
breadcrumbs and black pepper to taste
and mix to combine. Unroll loin and
spread with stuffing. Reroll and tie
securely with kitchen string.

2   To make glaze, place mustard,
barbecue sauce and tomato sauce in
a bowl, mix to combine and brush
over lamb.

3   Heat a microwave browning dish
on HIGH (100%) for 3 minutes. Place
lamb in centre of dish and roll to
brown outside and to seal. Cook on
HIGH (100%) for 3 minutes, then on
MEDIUM (50%) for 9 minutes.
Alternatively, brown meat in a frying
pan then transfer to a microwavable
dish and cook as directed.

4   Cover lamb with aluminium foil
and stand for 5 minutes.

Serves 2-3

Above: Peanut Beef Satay
Right: Veal Cacciatore

PEANUT BEEF SATAY

1 tablespoon peanut (groundnut) oil
1 onion, finely chopped
2 cloves garlic, crushed
1 teaspoon finely chopped fresh
red chilli
500 g/1 lb rump steak or silverside,
cut into thin strips
220 g/7 oz bottled satay stir-fry sauce
$^1/_2$ cup/125 mL/4 fl oz coconut milk
2 tablespoons lemon juice
250 g/8 oz green beans, halved
1 red pepper, thinly sliced

1 Place oil, onion, garlic and chilli
in a microwavable casserole dish,
cover and cook on HIGH (100%)
for 3 minutes.

2 Stir in beef, satay sauce, coconut
milk and lemon juice, cover and cook
for 5 minutes.

3 Add green beans and red pepper,
stir, cover and cook on MEDIUM (50%)
for 5 minutes or until vegetables are
tender crisp.

Serves 4

For a complete meal serve
with brown or white rice or
Oriental noodles.

VEAL CACCIATORE

1 eggplant (aubergine), cut into
1 cm/^{1}/$_2$ in cubes
1 clove garlic, crushed
^{1}/$_3$ cup/90 mL/3 fl oz French dressing
4 thin slices veal steak or schnitzel
(escalopes), cut into thin strips
500 mL/16 fl oz jar cacciatore or
similar tomato pasta sauce
8 green olives, sliced

1 Place eggplant (aubergine), garlic and dressing in a bowl and mix to combine.

2 Place veal around edge of a microwavable casserole dish and place eggplant (aubergine) in the centre, cover and cook on HIGH (100%) for 3 minutes.

3 Stir in sauce, cover and cook on MEDIUM (50%) for 5 minutes, stir, then cook for 5 minutes longer or until veal is cooked. Scatter with olives and serve immediately.

Serves 4

This is a quick version of a classic recipe which uses a good quality processed sauce to save time.
For a complete meal serve with pasta, noodles or rice and a tossed green salad.

Plate Villa Italiana

HERBED SAUSAGE CASSOULET

4 rashers bacon, cut into
2.5 cm/1 in strips
2 large onions, chopped
2 cloves garlic, crushed
375 g/12 oz smoked wurst sausage,
cut into thick slices
1 tablespoon chopped fresh marjoram
or oregano
440 g/14 oz canned tomatoes,
undrained and mashed
1 cup/250 mL/8 fl oz red wine
$^1/_2$ cup/125 mL/4 fl oz chicken stock
$^1/_3$ cup/90 mL/3 fl oz tomato paste
(purée)
440 g/14 oz canned haricot or
navy beans, rinsed and drained
1 large zucchini (courgette), sliced
chopped fresh parsley

1 Place bacon, onions and garlic in a
microwave browning casserole dish,
cover and cook on HIGH (100%)
for 2$^1/_2$ minutes, stir, then cook for
2$^1/_2$ minutes longer.

2 Add sausage and marjoram or
oregano to casserole, cover and cook
on MEDIUM (50%) for 3 minutes.

3 Stir in tomatoes, wine, stock and
tomato paste (purée), cover and cook
on HIGH (100%) for 8 minutes.

4 Stir in beans and zucchini
(courgette), cover and cook on
MEDIUM (50%) for 3 minutes.
Sprinkle with parsley and serve
immediately.

Serves 4

Serve with creamy mashed
or jacket baked potatoes.
Use any variety of thick
smoked sausage for this
hearty cassoulet.

BOLOGNESE SAUCE

2 rashers bacon, chopped
1 onion, finely chopped
1 clove garlic, crushed
2 tablespoons olive oil
500 g/1 lb lean beef mince
1 carrot, grated
1 stalk celery, thinly sliced
440 g/14 oz canned tomatoes,
undrained, cut in chunky pieces
$^1/_3$ cup/90 mL/3 fl oz tomato paste
(purée)
1 beef stock cube, crumbled
$^1/_4$ cup/60 mL/2 fl oz red wine,
(optional)
freshly ground black pepper
2 tablespoons chopped fresh parsley
or oregano

1 Place bacon, onion, garlic and oil in
a microwave browning casserole dish,
cover and cook on HIGH (100%) for
2 minutes, stir, then cook for 2 minutes
longer.

2 Stir in beef and spread out to make
an even layer, cover and cook for
3 minutes, stir and cook for 2 minutes
longer.

3 Add carrot, celery, tomatoes,
tomato paste (purée), stock cube,
wine, if using, and black pepper to
taste. Cover and cook for 15 minutes.
Stir in parsley or oregano and serve
immediately.

Serves 4

This popular and long-time
favourite cooks well and
speedily in the microwave.
Don't just keep it for serving
over pasta, it is also great
as a stuffing for vegetables,
as meat sauce for lasagne
and cannelloni or for
serving in tacos, crêpes or
cabbage rolls.

TASTY SIDES

Let your imagination run riot when you cook vegetables and grain dishes in the microwave. Vegetables retain their nutrients, colour and texture and interesting grain dishes can be cooked without fuss.

Here you will find exciting recipes for dishes such as Simple Risotto Milanese, Hungarian Mushroom Medley and Basque Ratatouille.

VEGETABLES WITH THREE CHEESES

2 bulbs fennel, trimmed and halved or
2 chokoes, peeled, halved and seeded
15 g/$^{1}/_{2}$ oz butter
12 spring onions, thinly sliced
100 g/3$^{1}/_{2}$ oz ricotta or cottage cheese, drained
60 g/2 oz Gorgonzola or soft blue cheese, crumbled
75 g/2$^{1}/_{2}$ oz grated Parmesan cheese

Serve as a stylish accompaniment to roast meat or as a vegetarian meal with brown rice. The stuffing is also good in zucchini (courgettes).

1   If using fennel, remove centre leaves to make a hollow for the stuffing. Place fennel or chokoes in two clean microwavable plastic bags. Twist neck of bag and fold under to seal. Place bags on opposite edges of turntable and cook on HIGH (100%) for 3-4 minutes, turn over and cook for 4 minutes longer or until vegetables are tender.

2   Melt butter in a microwavable bowl on MEDIUM (50%) for 1 minute. Add spring onions, cover and cook for 3 minutes. Stir in ricotta or cottage cheese, Gorgonzola or blue cheese and 60 g/2 oz Parmesan cheese and cook for 1 minute. Mix well to combine.

3   Spoon cheese mixture into centre of each fennel or choko half and place evenly around edge of turntable with thickest parts towards edge and cook on MEDIUM (50%) for 2 minutes.

4   Sprinkle with remaining Parmesan cheese and cook under a preheated hot grill for 3-4 minutes or until golden.

Serves 4

HUNGARIAN MUSHROOM MEDLEY

500 g/1 lb mixed mushrooms
30 g/1 oz butter
2 yellow or green peppers, thinly sliced
pinch sweet paprika
2 tablespoons lemon juice

Use any combination of fresh mushrooms available such as champignons, ceps, chanterelles, Roman brown, morels or any of the Asian varieties.
Serve mushrooms with eggs 'en cocotte' for a light main meal or they make a delicious accompaniment to grilled or pan-cooked meats or chicken.

1   Prepare mushrooms according to variety. Cut large mushrooms into thick slices and leave small ones whole.

2   Place butter and yellow or green peppers into a microwavable bowl, cover and cook on HIGH (100%) for 2 minutes, stir, then cook for 2 minutes longer.

3   Stir in mushrooms, paprika and lemon juice, cover and cook for 3 minutes, stir, then cook for 2 minutes longer or until mushrooms are tender.

Serves 4

SIMPLE RISOTTO MILANESE

Simple Risotto Milanese

60 g/2 oz butter
1 onion, diced
1 cup/220 g/7 oz long grain rice,
washed and drained
1 cup/250 mL/8 fl oz boiling chicken
stock, made with stock cubes
3/4 cup/185 mL/6 fl oz dry white wine
pinch saffron powder
60 g/2 oz grated Parmesan cheese

1   Place butter and onion in a
microwavable bowl and cook on
HIGH (100%) for 2 minutes. Stir well.

2   Stir in rice, stock, wine and saffron,
cover and cook for 10 minutes. Stand
for 4 minutes, stir in cheese and serve.

Serves 4

Patience is 'the order of the
day' when making a
traditional risotto but this
microwave version is made
in about half the time.
Serve sprinkled with
additional Parmesan
cheese and accompanied
by a green salad.

NAPOLITANA VEGETABLE SPAGHETTI

**1 large vegetable spaghetti or
spaghetti squash
2 tablespoons toasted pine nuts**

NAPOLITANA SAUCE
**2 onions, finely chopped
1 clove garlic, crushed
$^1/_4$ cup/60 mL/2 fl oz olive oil
1 kg/2 lb tomatoes, peeled and roughly
chopped or 2 x 440 g/14 oz canned
tomatoes, undrained and mashed
$^3/_4$ cup/185 mL/6 fl oz tomato paste
(purée)
2 tablespoons chopped fresh oregano
or marjoram
2 tablespoons shredded fresh basil
1 teaspoon sugar
freshly ground black pepper**

1   Cut squash into thirds and remove
seeds. Place squash in three clean
microwavable plastic bags. Twist neck
of bag and fold under squash. Place bags
evenly around edge of turntable
and cook on HIGH (100%) for
8-10 minutes or until squash is tender.
Set aside.

2   To make sauce, place onions, garlic
and oil in a microwavable bowl,
cover and cook on HIGH (100%) for
2 minutes, stir, then cook for 2 minutes
longer. Stir in tomatoes, cover and
cook for 4 minutes. Add tomato paste
(purée), oregano or marjoram, basil,
sugar and black pepper to taste, cover
and cook for 3 minutes, stir, then cook
for 3 minutes longer.

3   Tease squash strands out of skin,
using a fork and place in a warm
serving bowl. Spoon over sauce, toss to
combine and sprinkle with pine nuts.

Serves 6

The vegetable spaghetti or
spaghetti squash has long
strings or strands of flesh
inside which can be pulled
out of the cooked squash
with a fork. This vegetable
has a short season, but is
low in kilojoules (calories)
so is great for the slimmer
or health-conscious.
For a healthy and delicious
meal serve with a mixed
green salad and Italian
bread rolls.

STUFFED TOMATOES

**6 ripe tomatoes
salt
freshly ground black pepper**

MUSHROOM AND RICE STUFFING
**2 tablespoons olive oil
1 onion, diced
125 g/4 oz mushrooms, finely chopped
$^1/_2$ cup/100 g/3$^1/_2$ oz brown rice,
cooked
60 g/2 oz Brazil nuts or almonds,
chopped
3 tablespoons currants
1 tablespoon shredded fresh basil or
mint
2 tablespoons sour cream**

1   Cut a 'lid' from the top of each tomato
and using a teaspoon scoop out pulp and
reserve. Sprinkle tomato shells with salt
and black pepper and place upside down
on absorbent kitchen paper to drain.

2   To make stuffing, place oil and
onion into a microwavable bowl,
cover and cook on HIGH (100%) for
3 minutes. Stir in mushrooms, cover
and cook for 2 minutes. Add rice, nuts,
currants, basil or mint, sour cream and
reserved tomato pulp.

3   Place tomato shells in a shallow
microwavable dish. Fill with stuffing
and cook on MEDIUM (50%) for
5 minutes or until tomatoes are cooked
and stuffing is hot.

Serves 6

These tomatoes make a
delicious first course, an
unusual accompaniment
or a nourishing vegetarian
meal when served with a
green salad.
To cook brown rice in the
microwave, place 1 cup/
220 g/7 oz brown rice and
3 cups/750 mL/1$^1/_4$ pt water
in microwavable bowl or
jug and cook on HIGH
(100%) for 30-35 minutes or
until liquid is absorbed. Fluff
up with a fork and stand for
5 minutes before serving.

BASQUE RATATOUILLE

¹/4 cup/60 mL/2 fl oz olive oil
1 red onion, chopped
1 green or red pepper, thinly sliced
1 clove garlic, crushed
4 zucchini (courgettes), sliced
1 small eggplant (aubergine), cut into
1 cm/¹/2 in cubes
3 ripe tomatoes, cut into wedges
¹/4 cup/60 mL/2 fl oz dry sherry
¹/4 cup/60 mL/2 fl oz tomato paste
(purée)
3 tablespoons ground almonds
freshly ground black pepper

The French serve this as a hot vegetable stew or as a cold salad. It keeps well in the refrigerator for 2-3 days. This version has a little sherry and some ground almonds added to give a Spanish flavour. Delicious served hot with roast meat or chicken or cold as part of a salad buffet.

1   Heat oil in a microwavable shallow casserole on HIGH (100%) for 30 seconds, add onion, red or green pepper and garlic, cover and cook for 3 minutes, stir, then cook for 2 minutes longer.

2   Add zucchini (courgettes), cover and cook for 3 minutes. Add eggplant (aubergine), cover and cook for 3 minutes, stir, then cook for 2 minutes longer.

3   Stir in tomatoes, sherry and tomato paste (purée), cover and cook for 4 minutes, stir, then cook for 4 minutes longer. Stir in almonds and season to taste with black pepper.

Serves 6-8

COUSCOUS MARRAKECH

1 cup/185 g/6 oz couscous
1 cup/250 mL/8 fl oz boiling chicken
or vegetable stock, made with stock
cubes
3 spring onions, sliced
1 tablespoon olive oil
125 g/4 oz yellow squash, cut into
wedges or zucchini (courgettes), sliced
12 dessert prunes, pitted and
quartered
60 g/2 oz pistachio nuts, coarsely
chopped
2 teaspoons finely grated orange rind
2 tablespoons orange juice

The microwave is handy for heating savoury couscous dishes through before serving ensuring they are hot, but not dry or burnt. Serve with a lamb or chicken casserole, roast meat or as a vegetable dish for a vegetarian meal.

1   Place couscous in a microwavable bowl, pour over stock and toss with a fork. Cover and stand for 5 minutes or until liquid is absorbed.

2   Place spring onions and oil in a separate microwavable bowl, cover with a microwavable plate and set aside.

3   Place squash or zucchini (courgettes) in a clean microwavable plastic bag. Twist neck of bag and fold under vegetables to seal. Place bag on plate on top of bowl and cook on HIGH (100%) for 5 minutes.

4   Add spring onions, squash or zucchini (courgettes), prunes, nuts, orange rind and orange juice to couscous and mix to combine. Cover and cook on MEDIUM (50%) for 4 minutes or until heated through.

Serves 4

Couscous Marrakech

ASPARAGUS WITH TARRAGON CREAM

500 g/1 lb asparagus spears, trimmed

TARRAGON CREAM
1 egg
1 tablespoon caster sugar
1/4 cup/60 mL/2 fl oz tarragon vinegar
1/2 cup/125 mL/4 fl oz cream
(double), whipped
2 tablespoons chopped fresh dill or
snipped fresh chives

1   To make Tarragon Cream, place egg and sugar in a small microwavable bowl and beat until light and creamy. Beat in vinegar, 1 tablespoon at a time. Cook on MEDIUM (50%) for 1 minute, stir well and set aside to cool.

2   Fold cream and dill or chives into cold sauce.

3   Wash asparagus under cold running water, drain, shake off excess water and place in a clean microwavable plastic bag. Arrange spears loosely with tips altogether. Twist neck of bag and fold under asparagus to seal. Place bag on turntable with thick ends towards the edge and cook on HIGH (100%) for 3-5 minutes or until asparagus is just tender. Spoon sauce over hot asparagus and serve.

Serves 4

Asparagus retains its fresh summer green colour and subtle flavour when cooked in the microwave. This dish makes an elegant accompaniment to grilled fresh salmon or smoked salmon.

RED PESTO WITH PASTA

375 g/12 oz pasta of your choice,
freshly cooked
4 tablespoons grated Parmesan cheese

RED PESTO
1 large red pepper, quartered
30 g/1 oz sun-dried tomatoes in oil,
chopped and oil reserved
2 tablespoons pine nuts
2 cloves garlic, crushed
60 g/2 oz grated Parmesan cheese
1 tablespoon olive oil

For a complete meal serve with a tossed green salad. The microwave is a useful alternative to a grill to help you peel peppers for this delicious pasta sauce.

1   To make pesto, place red pepper into a clean microwavable plastic bag. Twist neck of bag and fold under red pepper to seal. Place bag on edge of turntable and cook on HIGH (100%) for 2 minutes. Stand for 5 minutes or until pepper is cool enough to handle. Using a small sharp knife and your fingers, remove skin from pepper.

2   Place red pepper, sun-dried tomatoes with oil, pine nuts and garlic in a food processor and process to make a rough textured paste. Add Parmesan cheese and oil and process briefly to combine.

3   Spoon pesto over hot pasta, sprinkle with Parmesan cheese and serve immediately.

Serves 4

TUSCANY BEAN SAUCE WITH PASTA

375 g/12 oz pasta of your choice,
freshly cooked
4 tablespoons pine nuts, toasted

TUSCANY BEAN SAUCE
125 g/4 oz shelled fresh or frozen
broad beans
30 g/1 oz anchovy fillets, drained and
chopped
2 cloves garlic, crushed
1 tablespoon olive oil
440 g/14 oz canned tomatoes, drained
and chopped
185 g/6 oz marinated artichokes,
drained and sliced
8 olives, pitted and sliced

For an easy and tasty meal serve accompanied with a tossed green salad.
For a more substantial dish stir 250 g/8 oz freshly cooked or canned mussels into the hot sauce just before serving.

1   Rinse broad beans under cold running water, drain and place in a clean microwavable plastic bag. Twist neck of bag and fold under beans. Place bag on edge of turntable and cook on HIGH (100%) for 1 minute.

2   Place anchovies, garlic and oil in a microwavable bowl, cover and cook on HIGH (100%) for 1 minute. Stir in tomatoes, artichokes, olives and broad beans, cover and cook on MEDIUM (50%) for 5 minutes or until hot.

3   Spoon sauce over hot pasta, sprinkle with pine nuts and serve immediately.

Serves 4

*Red Pesto with Pasta,
Tuscany Bean Sauce with Pasta*

Potatoes Karenina

4 red-skinned potatoes, about
750 g/1^1/2 lb, peeled
8 spring onions, thinly sliced
1 clove garlic, crushed
1 teaspoon vegetable oil
1 cup/250 g /8 oz cottage or
ricotta cheese, drained
1 cup/250 g/8 oz sour cream
60 g/2 oz grated tasty cheese
(mature Cheddar)
1 tablespoon soy grits or
steel cut oats (optional)
^{1}/4 teaspoon paprika

This delicious dish is a good side dish with baked ham or serve as a vegetarian meal accompanied by a mixed green salad.
Soy grits and steel cut oats are available from health food stores. They add a little colour and texture as well as food value to this dish.

Serves 4

1   Cut potatoes into quarters and place in a clean microwavable plastic bag. Twist neck of bag and fold under potatoes to seal. Place bag on edge of turntable, patting potatoes into an even layer and cook on HIGH (100%) for 7 minutes or until potatoes are just tender. Set aside until cool enough to handle, then cut into 2 cm/^{3}/4 in cubes.

2   Place spring onions, garlic and oil in a microwavable serving bowl, cover and cook for 3 minutes. Stir well.

3   Add potatoes, cottage or ricotta cheese and sour cream and mix gently to combine. Sprinkle with tasty cheese (mature Cheddar), soy grits or oats and paprika and cook on MEDIUM (50%) for 8 minutes.

Hot Potato Salad

4 red-skinned potatoes, about
750 g/1^1/2 lb
1 onion, diced
2 rashers bacon, chopped
2 tablespoons cornflour
1 cup/250 mL/8 fl oz vegetable stock
^{1}/4 cup/60 mL/2 fl oz cider or
tarragon vinegar
2 tablespoons wholegrain mustard
^{1}/3 cup/90 mL/3 fl oz cream (double)
freshly ground black pepper
snipped fresh chives

This is a good hot dish to serve at a salad buffet or barbecue. Flat oval-shaped potatoes seem to cook the most evenly in the microwave.

1   Using a sharp knife score around the circumference of each potato.

2   Place potatoes evenly around edge of turntable and cook on HIGH (100%) for 5 minutes, turn over and cook for 3-5 minutes longer or until potatoes are cooked. Set aside until cool enough to handle, then remove skin and cut potatoes into 1 cm/^{1}/2 in cubes.

3   Place onion and bacon in a microwavable bowl, cover and cook on HIGH (100%) for 3 minutes, stir, then cook for 2 minutes longer.

4   Stir in cornflour, stock and vinegar, cover and cook for 4 minutes. Add mustard, cream and potatoes and mix gently to combine. Cover and cook on MEDIUM (50%) for 2 minutes or until hot. Season to taste with black pepper and sprinkle with chives. Serve warm.

Serves 6

Potatoes Karenina, Hot Potato Salad

Green plate Janet Niven Antiques

SWEET DELIGHTS

With the help of your microwave, hot desserts with delicious sauces can be created in minutes, and succulent and refreshing fruits can be turned into wonderful treats. A festive Christmas Plum Pudding, an American Christmas Cake and easy Apricot and Almond Muffins are also included here. All will tempt you and are sure to delight family and friends.

CHOCOLATE HAZELNUT PUDDINGS

12 teaspoons lime marmalade, warmed
100 g/3^1/$_2$ oz dark cooking chocolate, broken into small pieces
4 eggs, separated
^{1}/$_2$ cup/100 g/3^1/$_2$ oz caster sugar
1 teaspoon vanilla essence
100 g/3^1/$_2$ oz hazelnuts, toasted and ground
1 cup/60 g/2 oz white breadcrumbs, made from stale bread

CHOCOLATE FUDGE SAUCE
100 g/3^1/$_2$ oz dark chocolate, broken into small pieces
1 tablespoon caster sugar
^{1}/$_2$ cup/125 mL/4 fl oz cream (single)
1 tablespoon orange-flavoured liqueur

This recipe makes twelve puddings, but hungry teenagers and men will probably eat two!
Take care when melting chocolate in the microwave as it holds its shape and can burn if overheated. Always stir before giving additional cooking time.

1   Prepare a six-hole microwavable muffin tray by brushing with melted butter and coating evenly with caster sugar. Place 1 teaspoon marmalade in each hole.

2   Melt chocolate in a microwavable bowl on DEFROST (30%) for 2 minutes, stir, then cook for 2 minutes longer, continue in this way until chocolate is completely melted.

3   Beat egg yolks and 60 g/2 oz sugar until thick and creamy. Stir in melted chocolate and vanilla essence.

4   Beat egg whites until soft peaks form. Then gradually beat in remaining sugar and continue beating until stiff peaks from. Fold egg white mixture, hazelnuts and breadcrumbs into chocolate mixture. Spoon half the mixture into prepared muffin tray and cook, elevated, on MEDIUM (50%) for 4 minutes. Cover and stand for 1 minute before turning out. Repeat with remaining mixture.

5   To make sauce, melt chocolate in a microwavable bowl as described in step 2. Stir in sugar and cool slightly. Add cream and liqueur and mix well to combine. Serve with puddings.

Makes 12

GRATINEE OF STONE FRUITS

500 g/1 lb apricots, cherries or plums or 4 ripe mangoes, nectarines or peaches, sliced
3 egg yolks
^{1}/$_4$ cup/60 g/2 oz caster sugar
^{1}/$_4$ teaspoon vanilla essence
1^1/$_4$ cups/315 mL/10 fl oz cream (single)
2 tablespoons sour cream
4 tablespoons coffee crystal sugar

1   Place fruit in an even layer in four individual round microwavable dishes.

2   Beat egg yolks, caster sugar and vanilla essence until light and creamy. Combine cream and sour cream in a microwavable bowl and heat on HIGH (100%) for 2 minutes. Using a balloon whisk, whisk warm cream mixture into egg yolk mixture. Spoon over fruit, sprinkle with coffee crystal sugar and cook puddings, one at a time, on HIGH (100%) for 1 minute, then on MEDIUM (50%) for 1 minute or until topping is set like a custard.

Serves 4

STICKY DATE PUDDING

3 fresh dates, pitted and quartered
155 g/5 oz pitted dates
1 cup/250 mL/8 fl oz boiling water
1 teaspoon bicarbonate of soda
60 g/2 oz unsalted butter, softened
³/4 cup/170 g/5¹/2 oz caster sugar
3 eggs
1¹/4 cups/155 g/5 oz self-raising flour
1 teaspoon vanilla essence

CARAMEL SAUCE
60 g/2 oz unsalted butter
¹/2 cup/90 g/3 oz brown sugar
¹/2 cup/125 mL/4 fl oz cream (single)
¹/4 cup/60 g/2 oz sour cream

1   Prepare a six-hole microwavable muffin tray by brushing with melted butter and coating evenly with caster sugar. Place a piece of fresh date in each hole.

2   Chop pitted dates and place in a microwavable bowl. Stir in boiling water and bicarbonate of soda and heat on HIGH (100%) for 30 seconds.

3   Place butter and caster sugar in a food processor and process until light and fluffy. With machine running, add eggs, one at a time, and process to combine. Add date mixture, flour and vanilla essence and using pulse button mix until just combined.

4   Spoon half the mixture into prepared muffin tray and cook, elevated, on MEDIUM (50%) for 4 minutes or until cooked. Cover and stand for 1 minute before turning out. Repeat with remaining mixture.

5   To make sauce, melt butter in a microwavable bowl on DEFROST (30%) for 2 minutes. Stir in brown sugar and cook on MEDIUM (50%) for 1 minute, stir, then cook for 1 minute longer. Stir in cream and sour cream and heat on DEFROST (30%) for 4 minutes or until sauce is warm, but not boiling. Serve with puddings.

Makes 12

For a truly memorable dessert serve with thick cream or vanilla ice cream. Allow one or two puddings per serving depending on appetites.

Sticky Date Pudding

Plate Villa Italiana

CHRISTMAS PLUM PUDDING

Its good to know that you can save time in the pre-Christmas rush by pre-cooking your Christmas pudding in the microwave. When serving for Christmas dinner, steam conventionally for at least 1 hour – the result will be a moist and delicious pudding – the longer you steam it, the darker it gets! To flame the pudding, heat $^1/_4$ cup/60 mL/2 fl oz brandy in a microwavable jug on MEDIUM (50%) for 1 minute, quickly pour over the hot pudding and ignite with a long match or taper.

On completion of cooking some puddings may look moist in the centre, but they continue to cook after they are removed from the microwave.
Leftover pudding reheats quickly and successfully. For best results heat one portion at a time on DEFROST (30%) for 3 minutes or until hot.

1 kg/2 lb seedless raisins
500 g/1 lb sultanas
500 g/1 lb currants
125 g/4 oz mixed peel
60 g/2 oz chopped, blanched almonds
$^2/_3$ cup/100 g/$3^1/_2$ oz dark brown sugar
$^1/_4$ cup/60 mL/2 fl oz brandy or sherry
250 g/8 oz unsalted butter
6 eggs, beaten
$^1/_2$ cup/125 mL/4 fl oz stout
2 teaspoons finely grated orange rind
2 tablespoons orange juice
2 cups/250 g/8 oz self-raising flour
1 teaspoon ground nutmeg
1 teaspoon mixed spice
6 cups/375 g/12 oz white breadcrumbs, made from stale bread
1 carrot, grated
1 cooking apple, peeled, cored and grated

1 Place raisins, sultanas, currants, mixed peel, almonds, sugar and brandy or sherry in a bowl and mix to combine.

2 Melt butter in a microwavable bowl on MEDIUM (50%) for 5 minutes. Stir in fruit mixture, then add eggs, stout, orange rind and orange juice and mix to combine.

3 Sift together flour, nutmeg and mixed spice. Add flour mixture, breadcrumbs, carrot and apple to fruit mixture and mix well to combine.

4 Prepare microwavable pudding bowls by lining base with a double thickness of greaseproof paper and brushing generously with melted butter. Divide mixture between bowls and press down firmly. Cover each pudding securely with microwavable plastic food wrap. Cook puddings, one at a time, on edge of turntable as directed below.

5 Allow puddings to cool completely before removing plastic wrap, then cover each pudding securely with a double, pleated layer of buttered greaseproof paper and a layer of aluminium foil. Secure with string and store puddings in the refrigerator until required.

6 Steam each pudding for at least 1 hour before turning out and serving.

Makes two 6 cup/1.5 litre/$2^1/_2$ pt puddings, three 4 cup/1 litre/$1^3/_4$ pt puddings or six 2 cup/500 mL/ 16 fl oz puddings

COOKING TIMES FOR PUDDINGS			
Bowl size	Power setting	Cooking time	No. servings per pudding
6 cup/1.5 litre/$2^1/_2$ pt	MEDIUM (50%) then on HIGH (100%)	15 minutes 3 minutes	12-16
4 cup/1 litre/$1^3/_4$ pt	MEDIUM (50%) then on HIGH (100%)	8 minutes 2 minutes	8-12
2 cup/500 mL/16 fl oz	MEDIUM (50%) then on HIGH (100%)	4 minutes 1 minute	4-6

Christmas Plum Pudding

Apricot and Almond Muffins

155 g/5 oz dried apricots, chopped
$^1/_2$ cup/90 g/3 oz brown sugar
45 g/1$^1/_2$ oz wheat germ
$^1/_4$ cup/30 g/1 oz rolled oats
3 tablespoons flaked almonds
$^1/_3$ cup/90 mL/3 fl oz vegetable oil
$^1/_4$ cup/60 mL/2 fl oz milk
2 eggs, lightly beaten
1 cup/125 g/4 oz self-raising flour
2 teaspoons ground cinnamon

ALMOND COCONUT TOPPING
3 tablespoons flaked almonds
3 tablespoons shredded coconut
3 tablespoons rolled oats

Serve muffins warm with yogurt and fresh fruit for a weekend breakfast or with mascarpone and berries for morning coffee.
Microwaved muffins are best eaten when freshly made, however any leftovers may be reheated and 'refreshed' later by heating on DEFROST (30%) for 1 minute.

1 To make topping, place almonds, coconut and rolled oats in a shallow microwavable dish and cook on HIGH (100%), stirring several times, for 2 minutes or until ingredients are golden in colour.

2 Place apricots, sugar, wheat germ, rolled oats, almonds, oil, milk and eggs in a bowl and mix to combine.

3 Sift flour and cinnamon into mixture and mix gently to combine.

4 Spoon half the mixture into a six-hole microwavable muffin tray. Sprinkle with half the topping and cook, elevated, on HIGH (100%) for 3 minutes. Turn onto a wire rack to cool. Repeat to use remaining mixture.

Makes 12

Left: Apricot and Almond Muffins
Above: Winter Fruit Crumble

WINTER FRUIT CRUMBLE

3 red-skinned apples, about 500 g/1 lb,
cored, peeled and sliced
2 kiwifruit, sliced
2 passion fruit
1 tablespoon sugar
2 tablespoons water

CRUMBLE TOPPING
$^1/_2$ cup/75 g/2$^1/_2$ oz wholemeal flour
60 g/2 oz unsalted butter, chopped
4 slices pumpernickel bread, about
125 g/4 oz, made into crumbs
2 tablespoons brown sugar
3 tablespoons soy grits or rolled oats

1   Place apples, kiwifruit, passion fruit
and sugar in a microwavable serving
dish, mix to combine and sprinkle with
water. Cover and cook on HIGH (100%)
for 5 minutes.

2   To make topping, place flour and
butter in a food processor and process
for 20 seconds or until mixture
resembles fine breadcrumbs. Transfer
mixture to a bowl. Add breadcrumbs,
brown sugar and soy grits or rolled oats
and mix to combine. Sprinkle topping
over fruit and cook on MEDIUM (50%)
for 5 minutes.

Serves 4

The nutty flavour and
texture of pumpernickel
breadcrumbs complements
the sweetness of fresh
winter fruits in this lovely
pudding.
The crumble is delicious
served with vanilla ice
cream or whipped cream.
For something different, try
using pears, quinces or
nashi fruit in place of the
apples.

GINGERBREAD PUDDING

1 cup/125 g/4 oz self-raising flour
1 teaspoon ground ginger
$^1/_2$ teaspoon ground cinnamon
2 cups/250 g/8 oz coarse oatmeal
90 g/3 oz unsalted butter
$^1/_2$ cup/170 g/5$^1/_2$ oz golden syrup
1 cup/170 g/5$^1/_2$ oz brown sugar
1 egg, beaten
$^1/_4$ cup/60 mL/2 fl oz milk
icing sugar, sifted

Serve this spicy pudding with Apricot Sauce and cinnamon-flavoured cream. Coarse oatmeal is available from health food shops and some supermarkets – it gives the pudding an interesting texture.

1 Sift flour, ginger and cinnamon together into a bowl. Stir in oatmeal and make a well in the centre.

2 Place butter, golden syrup and sugar in a microwavable bowl or jug and heat on HIGH (100%) for 1 minute, stir, then heat for 1 minute longer or until mixture is melted.

3 Pour butter mixture and egg into well in centre of dry ingredients and mix to combine. Stir in milk.

4 Pour mixture into a greased 6 cup/ 1.5 litre/2$^1/_2$ pt capacity microwavable kugelhopf or fluted ring mould and cook, elevated, on MEDIUM (50%) for 7-8 minutes or until pudding is cooked. Cover and stand for 2 minutes. Remove cover and cool on a rack until firm around the edges. Turn out, sprinkle with icing sugar and serve warm.

Serves 8

APRICOT SAUCE

250 g/8 oz dried apricots
2 cups/500 mL/16 fl oz boiling water
$^1/_3$ cup/90 mL/3 fl oz orange juice
$^1/_4$ cup/60 mL/2 fl oz brandy

1 Place apricots and water in a microwavable bowl or jug, cover and cook on HIGH (100%) for 8 minutes or until apricots are tender. Set aside to cool.

2 Place apricot mixture in a food processor or blender and process to make a purée. Add orange juice and brandy and mix to combine.

3 Place apricot purée in a microwavable bowl or jug and heat on HIGH (100%) for 2-3 minutes or until sauce is hot.

Makes 2 cups/500 mL/16 fl oz

Serve this delicious sauce with Gingerbread Pudding, crêpes or over ice cream.

Gingerbread Pudding, Apricot Sauce

*Above: Rhubarb and Strawberry
Crumble*
Right: American Christmas Cake

RHUBARB AND STRAWBERRY CRUMBLE

500 g/1 lb rhubarb, trimmed and pink
parts only cut into 2.5 cm/1 in pieces
$^1/_4$ cup/45 g/1$^1/_2$ oz brown sugar
250 g/8 oz strawberries, quartered or
halved

MUESLI CRUMBLE TOPPING
$^1/_2$ cup/75 g/2$^1/_2$ oz wholemeal flour
60 g/2 oz unsalted butter, cubed
$^1/_2$ cup/100 g/3$^1/_2$ oz toasted muesli
1 tablespoon wheat germ
1 tablespoon burghul (cracked wheat)
$^1/_2$ teaspoon ground nutmeg

Stewed rhubarb and fresh
strawberries are a delicious
and colourful combination
in this superb dessert.
Serve crumble hot with
thick cream, vanilla ice
cream or mascarpone.

1   Place rhubarb into a microwavable
dish, sprinkle with sugar, cover and
cook on HIGH (100%) for 3 minutes,
stir, then cook for 2 minutes longer.
Scatter strawberries over cooked
rhubarb.

2   To make topping, place flour and
butter in a food processor and process
for 30 seconds or until mixture
resembles fine breadcrumbs. Add
muesli, wheat germ, burghul (cracked
wheat) and nutmeg and using the pulse
process briefly to combine.

3   Sprinkle topping over fruit and cook
on MEDIUM (50%) for 5 minutes.

Serves 6

AMERICAN CHRISTMAS CAKE

185 g/6 oz whole Brazil nuts
185 g/6 oz whole pecans
185 g/6 oz seedless raisins
125 g/4 oz dessert dates, pitted
125 g/4 oz glacé red cherries
125 g/4 oz glacé green cherries
125 g/4 oz mixed peel
$^2/_3$ cup/100 g/3$^1/_2$ oz dark brown sugar
$^3/_4$ cup/90 g/3 oz flour
$^1/_2$ teaspoon baking powder
4 eggs, beaten
1 tablespoon brandy
1 egg white, lightly beaten

Makes a 23 cm/9 in ring cake

1   Line the base of a 23 cm/9 in microwavable ring mould with greaseproof paper and brush generously with melted butter.

2   Place Brazil nuts, pecans, raisins, dates, red cherries, green cherries, mixed peel and sugar into a bowl and mix to combine.

3   Sift flour and baking powder over fruit mixture, then add eggs and brandy and mix to combine.

4   Spoon mixture into prepared ring mould and press down firmly. Cook, elevated, on MEDIUM (50%) for 20-25 minutes or until cooked when tested with a skewer. Cover and stand for 5 minutes. Brush top of cake with egg white and leave to cool in mould.

This cake is dense with nuts and fruit and should be served in thin slices. It is a traditional American festive cake and is not usually iced so is another fuss-free recipe. Store in an airtight container until ready to serve.

Gift box on left Orson and Blake

71

Passionfruit
Cheese

SPECIAL TREATS

Tempting treats for chocoholics, a mulled wine and an exotic Camembert cheese – great fare for your next party – are all quick and easy to prepare with some help from your microwave.

Pretty jars of unusual preserves, such as Berry and Rose Conserve and Passion Fruit Cheese, make wonderful gifts.

Previous pages: Berry and Rose Conserve, Lime Curd; Cape Gooseberry Conserve, Passion Fruit Cheese (page 80)

BERRY AND ROSE CONSERVE

500g/1 lb strawberries or raspberries
or a mixture of both
^{1}/4 cup/60 mL/2 fl oz lemon juice
2 cups/500 g/1 lb sugar
3 teaspoons pectin
1 tablespoon rosewater

The microwave is handy for making small quantities of summer berry conserve and helps keep the heat out of the kitchen. The addition of rosewater, which is available from health food stores, makes this conserve very special.

Makes 2^1/2 cups /600 mL/1 pt

1   Wash strawberries, drain well and hull. Do not wash raspberries but 'pick over' to check for and remove bugs. Cut small strawberries in half and large ones into quarters. Leave raspberries whole.

2   Place berries and lemon juice in a large microwavable bowl or jug, cover and cook on HIGH (100%) for 5 minutes or until fruit is pulpy.

3   Stir in sugar and pectin and cook, uncovered for 2^1/2 minutes, stir, then cook for 2^1/2 minutes longer.

4   Stir in rosewater and pour conserve into hot sterilised jars. Seal when cold.

LIME CURD

125 g/4 oz unsalted butter, cubed
1 cup/220 g/7 oz caster sugar
finely grated rind of 6 limes
^{3}/4 cup /185 mL/6 fl oz lime juice
6 large egg yolks, beaten

A delicious and delightful variation of the popular lemon curd, also known as lemon cheese.

1   Place butter and sugar in a large microwavable jug and heat on MEDIUM (50%) for 1 minute, stir, then heat for 1 minute longer or until butter melts. Continue cooking in this way for 2 minutes longer or until sugar dissolves.

2   Stir in lime rind and lime juice. Add egg yolks and cook for 1 minute, stir well, then cook for 1 minute longer. Continue cooking in this way for 2 minutes longer or until mixture thickens. Pour curd into hot sterilised jars. Seal when cold and store in the refrigerator.

Makes 2^1/2 cups/600 mL/1 pt

Chocolate Shortcake

CHOCOLATE SHORTCAKE

200 g/6$^{1}/_{2}$ oz dark cooking chocolate,
broken into small pieces
100 g/3$^{1}/_{2}$ oz shortbread finger
biscuits, cut into chunky pieces
$^{1}/_{2}$ cup/125 g/4 oz sour cream or
$^{1}/_{2}$ cup/125 mL/4 fl oz cream (double)
$^{1}/_{2}$ cup/60 g/2 oz ground almonds or
hazelnuts
1 tablespoon orange-flavoured or
whiskey liqueur (optional)

1   Melt chocolate in a microwavable
bowl on DEFROST (30%) for
2 minutes, stir, then heat for 2 minutes
longer. Continue in this way for
6-8 minutes longer or until chocolate is
completely melted.

2   Stir shortbread into chocolate, then
add sour cream or cream, almonds or
hazelnuts and liqueur, if using, and mix
well to combine.

3   Press mixture in a base-lined and
buttered 18 cm/7 in diameter round
cake tin and chill until firm.

Makes an 18 cm/7 in round cake

This is a quick and slick treat
for chocoholics who don't
want to spend a lot of time
in the kitchen. Serve cut
into wedges for morning
coffee or afternoon tea or
with sugared berries for a
simple dessert.

Plates *Swid Powell* from Bibelot

CAMEMBERT TREAT

This is a novel way to serve Camembert cheese for a party. It is delicious served with a garnish of salad greens accompanied by oatmeal biscuits.
The microwave is used to 'ripen' the cheese and helps develop and blend the flavours. To serve a larger number of people use several Camembert cheeses rather than buy a bigger one which is trickier to soften evenly into the centre.

200-250 g/6^1/2-8 oz whole Camembert cheese
60 g/2 oz sun-dried tomatoes in oil, well drained
1 tablespoon chopped fresh oregano
1 tablespoon chopped fresh basil
60 g/2 oz marinated eggplant (aubergine) in oil, well drained

Serves 6-8

1 Cut Camembert cheese in half horizontally and place bottom half on a microwavable serving plate.

2 Top with sun-dried tomatoes, then sprinkle with oregano and basil and top with eggplant (aubergine). Cover with top half of Camembert cheese.

3 Cover Camembert cheese with microwavable plastic food wrap, place in centre of turntable and heat on DEFROST (30%) for 4 minutes or until cheese is soft and ripened in centre.

MULLED WINE

8 cups/2 litres/3^1/2 pt claret
^{1}/3 cup/90 mL/3 fl oz lemon juice
1 cinnamon stick
6 cloves
^{1}/4 teaspoon ground nutmeg
125 g/4 oz sugar cubes
^{1}/4 cup/60 mL/2 fl oz brandy
1 orange, thinly sliced
1 lemon, thinly sliced

Serves 12

1 Place claret, lemon juice, cinnamon, cloves and nutmeg in a microwavable bowl or jug, cover and heat on HIGH (100%) for 8 minutes, stir, then heat for 7 minutes longer or until boiling.

2 Place a wire cooling rack over bowl or jug and arrange sugar cubes in a circle.

3 Warm brandy in a microwavable jug, bowl or cup on HIGH (100%) for 30 seconds. Quickly pour hot brandy over sugar and ignite with a taper or long match. The sugar will dissolve, drip into the wine and sweeten it!

4 Add orange and lemon slices and mix to combine. To serve, ladle into mugs or glasses containing a metal teaspoon to prevent cracking and enjoy!

This drink gives you a warm glowing sensation on a cold night and is well known to snow skiers as 'gluewein'. It's easy to make in the microwave. Lemonade may be added to dilute the mulled wine.

Mulled Wine, Camembert Treat

EASTER CHOCOLATE TREATS

250 g/8 oz dark or milk chocolate,
broken into small pieces
2 teaspoons white vegetable
shortening or fat (optional), chopped
4 Easter bunny moulds, with a
capacity of about 30 mL/1 fl oz
4 Easter egg moulds, measuring
about 7.5 x 5 cm/3 x 2 in

Get the children to help
you make these Easter
bunnies and Easter eggs.
You will be delighted at the
fun you create but do wear
brown aprons! Do not use
compound chocolate for
these Easter delights.

1 Place chocolate and shortening or
fat, if using, in a microwavable bowl
and melt on DEFROST (30%) for
2 minutes, stir, then heat for 2 minutes
longer. Continue in this way until
chocolate is completely melted.

2 Carefully spoon or pour melted
chocolate into bunny moulds, then tap
gently on a firm surface to remove air
bubbles. Cover moulds and chill in
freezer until firm.

3 Place 2 tablespoons melted
chocolate into one half of an Easter egg
mould, then using paper clips secure
other half of mould over top. Turn
mould over, tilting and twisting until
mould is evenly coated with chocolate.
Shake mould well to ensure an even
coating. Place mould in freezer for
1 minute, turn over and freeze for
1 minute longer. Turn again and freeze
for 3 minutes or until chocolate is quite
firm. Repeat to make four Easter eggs.

4 To remove bunnies from moulds,
turn onto a bed of absorbent kitchen
paper. To remove Easter eggs, remove
paper clips and gradually ease
chocolate eggs away from moulds and
onto a bed of absorbent kitchen paper.
Store Easter bunnies and eggs in an
airtight container in a cool, dry place
until required.

*Makes 4 Easter bunnies and
4 Easter eggs*

CHOCOLATE-DIPPED FRUITS

60 g/2 oz dark or milk chocolate,
broken in small pieces
12 large strawberries
12 rambutans or lychees

Summer fruits dipped in
melted chocolate satisfies
the craving that some of us
have to finish a gourmet
meal with something sweet.
The combination of
chocolate and fruit is
surprisingly refreshing. Use
your imagination and try
other favourite fruits.

1 Melt chocolate in a microwavable
bowl on DEFROST (30%) for
2 minutes, stir, then heat for 2 minutes
longer. Continue in this way until
chocolate is completely melted.

2 Wash and dry strawberries, but do
not hull. Remove two-thirds of the
rambutan or lychee skin from top of
fruit leaving bottom to hold on to.

3 Holding strawberries by stalks and
rambutans or lychees by remaining
skin, carefully dip fruit one at a time
into chocolate to half coat. Place on
baking paper on a wire rack and leave
until chocolate sets.

4 To serve, place chocolate-dipped
fruits in petit four cases and serve
with after-dinner coffee, as a special
sweetmeat at a picnic or use to
decorate your favourite chocolate cake.

Makes 24

Easter Chocolate Treats, Chocolate-dipped Fruits

PASSION FRUIT CHEESE

125 g/4 oz unsalted butter, chilled
1 cup/220 g/7 oz caster sugar
1 cup/250 mL/8 fl oz passion fruit
pulp
6 large egg yolks

1   Place butter and sugar in a large microwavable jug and heat on MEDIUM (50%) for 1 minute, stir, then heat for 1 minute longer or until butter melts. Continue cooking in this way for 2 minutes longer or until sugar dissolves.

2   Add passion fruit pulp and stir well. Stir in egg yolks and cook for 1 minute, stir well, then cook for 1 minute longer. Continue cooking in this way for 6 minutes longer or until mixture thickens. Pour into hot sterilised jars. Seal when cold and store in the refrigerator.

Makes 2^1/2 cups/600 mL/1 pt

Try this tasty spread in the bottom of a soufflé dish when making a vanilla soufflé or as a filling with cream for a sponge cake.

CAPE GOOSEBERRY CONSERVE

250 g/8 oz cape gooseberries
2 tablespoons lemon juice
1 tablespoon orange flower water
1 cup/250 g/8 oz sugar
2 teaspoons pectin

1   Wash and dry gooseberries and cut in half. Place gooseberries, lemon juice and orange flower water in a large microwavable jug, cover and cook on HIGH (100%) for 5 minutes or until fruit is pulpy.

2   Stir in sugar and pectin and cook, uncovered, for 5 minutes. Pour into hot sterilised jars. Seal when cold.

Makes 1^1/4 cups/315 mL/10 fl oz

The cape gooseberry, also known as the strawberry tomato, ground cherry, tomatillo, dwarf cape gooseberry or Chinese lantern has a very short season, but you can enjoy their delicious flavour out of season in this wonderful conserve.